DISCOVER
BLUES IMPROVISATION

AN INTRODUCTION TO BLUES PIANO

KEYBOARD DISCOVERY LIBRARY

By Nancy & Randall Faber
with Edwin McLean

Contents

An alphabetical listing of pieces is on the inside back cover.

Production: Frank & Gail Hackinson
Production Coordination & Text Design: Marilyn Cole
Editor: Linda Witchie
Cover & Illustrations: Terpstra Design, San Francisco
Engraving: GrayBear Music Company, Hollywood, Florida

My baby, she done left me,
Took off on the mornin' train.
I said my baby, she done left me,
Took off on that mornin' train.
I feel so low-down deep inside,
Like I was wearin' a ball and chain.

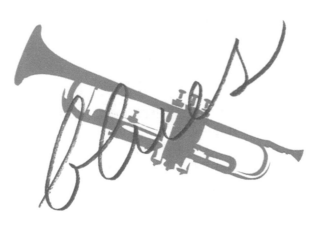

Story of the Blues

Everybody gets the blues once in awhile—you know what it feels like. If you live in the United States, you also know what it sounds like. Almost any singer could take the lyrics above and do 12 bars. The melody might be different, but the feel would be the same: rather slow, swing-style, and with plenty of feeling.

That feeling is uniquely American, or to be more precise, African-American. The blues grew out of the work songs and spirituals sung by black farm workers in the deep South, all the way back to when they were slaves. The blues was a language used to express their suffering, tell stories, and reveal their hopes and dreams.

Early blues artists were usually singers who accompanied themselves on the guitar or piano. During the early years of the phonograph, some of these artists became famous from their recordings: Leadbelly, Blind Lemon Jefferson, Ma Rainey, Bessie Smith, and others.

An important landmark in blues piano came in 1914, when W.C. Handy's famous *St. Louis Blues* was published. This song and others that Handy wrote were important in popularizing the blues. In the 1930's, boogie-woogie—a piano style featuring fancy left-hand patterns—reached its peak in popularity. Rhythm and blues caught on in the 1940's and later developed into rock 'n' roll and soul music.

Blues has influenced all kinds of music, from the big bands of the 20's and 30's (Count Basie, Duke Ellington), to cool jazz in the 50's (Miles Davis, the Modern Jazz Quartet), up to today's rock, heavy metal, and rap. Styles may have changed, but somehow the blues always stays the same. So it's no surprise that when musicians come together to jam for the first time, they always play that universal language—the blues!

Preparing for the Blues

Half Step

On the keyboard, a half step is the distance from one key to the **very next key.**

1. Find and play these **half steps** on the piano.
   Say aloud "half step" as you play.

   A **half step** is a **minor 2nd.**

Whole Step

A **whole step** is made up of 2 half steps.
On the keyboard, a whole step is formed by 2 keys with **one key in between.**

2. Find and play these **whole steps** on the piano.
   Say aloud "whole step" as you play.

   A **whole step** is a **major 2nd.**

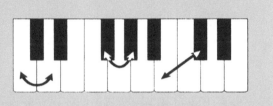

The Major Scale

The C major scale has 7 tones—**C D E F G A B (C)**

3a. Mark **W** for whole steps and **H** for half steps for the C major scale below.

b. Then write **M2** (Major 2nd) or **m2** (minor 2nd) for each interval.

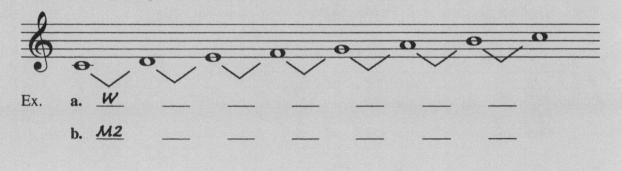

Ex. a. *W* ___ ___ ___ ___ ___ ___

     b. *M2* ___ ___ ___ ___ ___ ___

Note: The above concepts are explored with improvisational exercises in *Discover Beginning Improvisation*.

Swing is the Thing

1. Play this 5-finger scale with **straight rhythm**—even 8th notes.

Mo - zart, Bach, and Bee - tho - ven are great. *2 - 3 - 4*
Eighth notes played in clas - sic style are straight. *2 - 3 - 4*

Play it again while tapping your L.H. in your lap on beats 1 - 2 - 3 - 4.

One of the things that makes the blues sound so different from the classical music of Mozart and Beethoven is the use of **swing rhythm**.

Swing Rhythm

In swing rhythm, 8th notes are played in a *long-short* pattern.

2. Clap these 8th notes with your teacher, using a *long-short* **swing rhythm**.

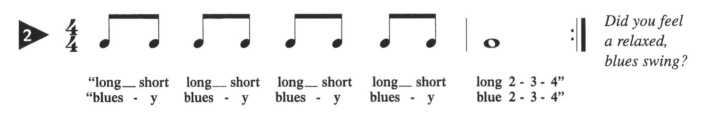

Did you feel a relaxed, blues swing?

"long— short   long— short   long— short   long— short   long 2 - 3 - 4"
"blues - y   blues - y   blues - y   blues - y   blue 2 - 3 - 4"

3. Now play the 5-finger scale in **swing rhythm**—*long-short* 8th notes.

Swing the 8ths!

When you play the blues, it's got - ta swing. *2 - 3 - 4*
Feel the groove 'cause swing - in' is the thing. *2 - 3 - 4*

Play it again while tapping your L.H. in your lap on beats 1 - 2 - 3 - 4.

Play each of these famous melodies in two rhythm styles:
1) **straight rhythm** (as written)
2) **swing rhythm** (*long-short* 8th notes)

Notice how swing rhythm changes the *feel* of the melody.

Dance Hall of the Mountain King

4. Play *straight*; repeat with *swing*.

adapted from Grieg

Teacher Part:

A Swingin' Musette

5. Play *straight*; repeat with *swing*.

adapted from Bach

Teacher Part:

Important Note: Use swing rhythm for all of the pieces and exercises in this blues book, unless otherwise noted.

Some of the students play the melodies above, while others clap as follows:
- For *straight style,* clap on **beats 1** and **3.**
- For *swing style,* clap on **beats 2** and **4.**

Woodsheddin'

Blues Talk: *I put in my hours back at the shed.*
Got the blues in my soul,
And the sounds in my head.

Famous blues players would practice for hours
in such humble places as an old woodshed.

The saying "woodshed your part" means:
Practice hard on your own!

1. "Woodshed" this exercise to build your blues
   technique. Enjoy the feel of **swing rhythm**!

Back at the Shed

In swing

Swing- in' with some feel - in' in   the   old wood - shed. Swing- in' with some feel - in' in the   old wood - shed.

Swing- in' with some feel - in' in   the   old wood - shed. Swing- in' with some feel - in' in   the   old wood - shed.

Swing- in' with some feel - in' in   the   old wood - shed. Swing- in' with some feel - in' in   the   old wood - shed.

2. Play *Back at the Shed* **hands together**
   with your L.H. playing one octave lower.

   Try these 3 tempos with the teacher duet:
   Notice the mood of each new tempo.

▷ **7** ▶ Slow lazy blues ♩ = 64

▷ **8** ▶ Cool moderate swing ♩ = 100

▷ **9** ▶ Saturday night swing ♩ = 132

Teacher Part: (Student plays as written)

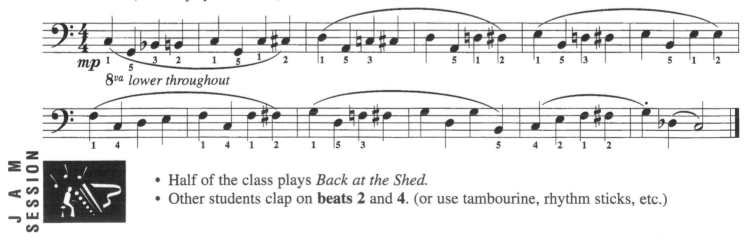

8va lower throughout

J A M   S E S S I O N

- Half of the class plays *Back at the Shed.*
- Other students clap on **beats 2** and **4.** (or use tambourine, rhythm sticks, etc.)

FF1

Blues Talk: *When I opened my ears*
I heard the blues
From the top of my head
To the holes in my shoes.

Your teacher will play a musical example. Close your eyes while you listen.

Does the music use **straight rhythm** or **swing rhythm**? Circle your answer.

1. *straight*	**2.** *straight*	**3.** *straight*
or	or	or
swing	*swing*	*swing*

4. *straight*	**5.** *straight*	**6.** *straight*
or	or	or
swing	*swing*	*swing*

For Teacher Use Only (The examples may be played in any order.)

Exploring the 12-Bar Blues in C

The blues often uses three chords built on **steps 1, 4,** and **5** of the major scale.

The Roman numerals **I, IV,** and **V** are used to name these chords.

1. Play the chords below with your left hand.

Say aloud, "**I chord**," "**IV chord**," or "**V chord**."

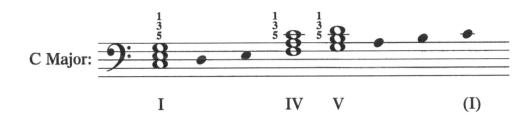

C Major:

I   IV   V   (I)

The 12-Bar Blues

To blues players, the word *bar* means measure.
The **12-bar blues** is a repeating 12-measure pattern of chords (chord progression).
It can be played with the 3 chords you just learned: **I, IV,** and **V.**

2. Practice the 12-bar blues **chord progression** below.

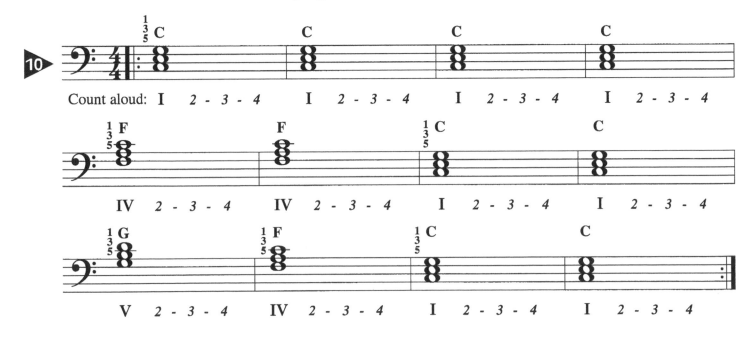

Play *The 12-Bar Blues* as an ensemble, with each player's part in a different octave.
• Bass Part: Play only the **root** in a low octave.
• Accompaniment Part I: Play open **5ths** with the left hand.
• Accompaniment Part II: Play **3-note chords** with the right hand.

FF1

The 12-bar blues can be shown like this:

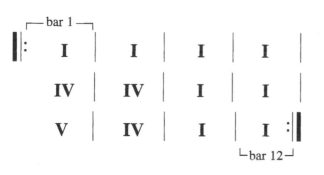

Roman Numeral Blues

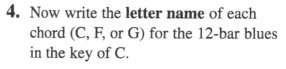

11 ▶ **1.** Play *The 12-Bar Blues* (p. 8) looking *only* at the Roman numerals above.
   Hint: Count to 4 for each left-hand chord! (Your teacher may play the duet shown below.)

2. Now **memorize** the 12-bar blues pattern and play it for your teacher.
   Can you play it by memory while your teacher plays the duet part below?

3. Complete the 12-bar-blues by writing the correct **Roman numeral** inside each box. (Cover up the top of the page.)

4. Now write the **letter name** of each chord (C, F, or G) for the 12-bar blues in the key of C.

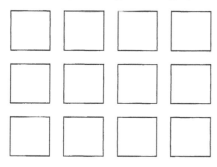

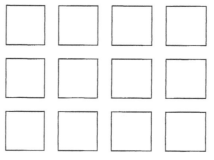

Teacher Part: (This bass line may be played while the student is learning the blues progression.)

- Teacher writes the 12-bar blues pattern on the board with errors. Students take turns correcting.
- Time students as they write the 12-bar blues pattern with **Roman numerals** (I, IV, V).
- Time students writing the 12-bar blues pattern with **chord names** (C, F, G) in the key of C.

Blues Technique

Woodsheddin'

In the early 1900s, blues pianists sometimes performed in shacks called barrelhouses.

The *barrelhouse* piano style has a steady, repeating **left-hand pattern**.

Barrelhouse Blues

First "woodshed" the **left hand alone**. Practice for smooth hand position changes.
Then practice slowly hands together. *Listen* for a steady beat!

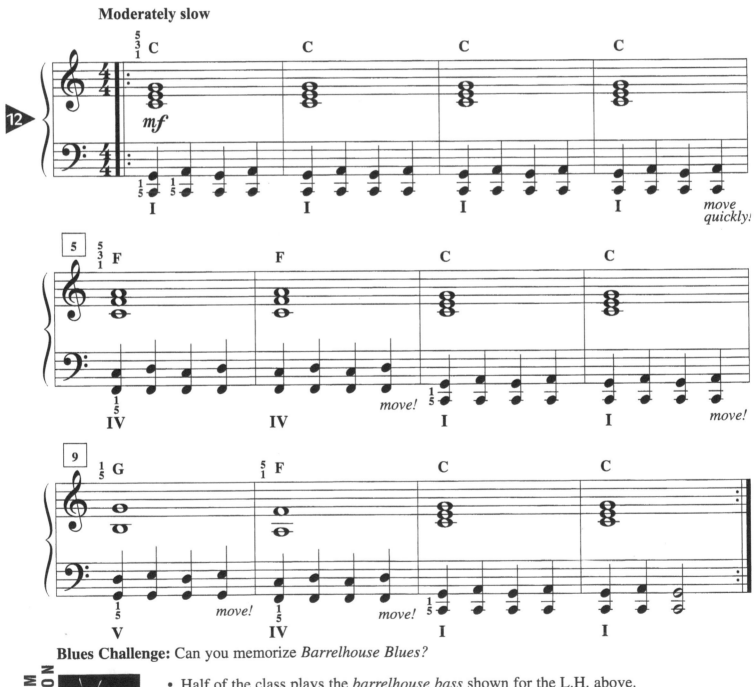

Blues Challenge: Can you memorize *Barrelhouse Blues*?

JAM SESSION

- Half of the class plays the *barrelhouse bass* shown for the L.H. above.
- The other students play R.H. chords in root position (C, F, or G) on *beat 1* of each measure. Then reverse the groups.

FF11

When reading music, you should always know where you are on the page.

When playing the blues, you should always know where you are in the
12-bar blues **chord progression**.

Your teacher will begin playing the 12-bar blues and **stop** on one of the chords.
Close your eyes, *listen,* then circle the *last* chord your teacher plays.

1. C   C   C   C
    F   F   C   C
    G   F   C   C

2. I   I   I   I
    IV IV I   I
    V   IV I   I

3. C   C   C   C
    F   F   C   C
    G   F   C   C

4. C   C   C   C
    F   F   C   C
    G   F   C   C

5. C   C   C   C
    F   F   C   C
    G   F   C   C

6. I   I   I   I
    IV IV I   I
    V   IV I   I

For Teacher Use Only Begin playing the 12-bar blues, then stop on the *downbeat* of any measure.

Play at slow, moderate, and fast tempos.

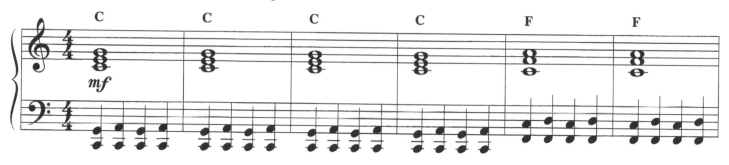

- Students write the 12-bar-blues progression on the board.
  Use chord names or Roman numerals.

- One student plays *Barrelhouse Blues* (p.10), stopping on any chord in the 12-bar pattern.
  Other students circle the last harmony heard. Repeat with a new student playing.

Exploring the Minor 3rd

There are two kinds of **2nds**—the **minor 2nd** and the **major 2nd.**

Find and play: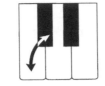

A minor 2nd is a **half step.**
(*minor* means smaller)

Find and play:

A major 2nd is a **whole step.**
(*major* means larger)

There are also two kinds of **3rds**—the **minor 3rd** and the **major 3rd.**

Find and play:

A **minor 3rd** spans a
whole step plus a half step.

Find and play:

A **major 3rd** spans
two whole steps.

The sound of the minor 3rd is an important part of the blues!

Swinging the Minor 3rd

1. Play this short **minor 3rd** melody (C to E♭) using *swing rhythm.*

When you play the blues it's got - ta swing! *2 - 3 - 4*

Repeat in
higher octaves.

2. Now play the same melody using different **minor 3rds**. (Repeat in higher octaves.)

- **G**, up a minor 3rd to **B♭**.
- **D**, up a minor 3rd to **F**.
- **F**, up a minor 3rd to _____(?).
- **A**, up a minor 3rd to _____(?).

FF1

Bluesy Minor 3rds

- The L.H. plays only C and G (scale steps 1 and 5).
- The R.H. plays C and G with **minor 3rds** (C - E♭ and G - B♭).

When the Blues is Callin'

Remember to swing the 8th notes!

N. Faber

Extra Credit: Can you create your own version of *When the Blues is Callin'?*
Use C and G for the L.H. Use the minor 3rds C - E♭ and G - B♭ to create your R.H. melody.

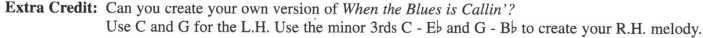

Improvise — means to create "on the spot."

Improvise your own R.H. "train whistle" at the end of this piece.
Use the minor 3rds: **C - E♭** or **G - B♭.**

Enjoy this barrelhouse blues!

Blues Train

N. and R. Faber

Moderate blues

(The train is leaving town)

Improvise on C and E♭
Improvise on G and B♭
Improvise on high C and E♭

- Play *Blues Train* as a class, assigning students the treble or bass part.
  (For digital pianos, use different keyboard settings.)

- Keep repeating the piece, with each student improvising a solo for measures 13-18.

JAM SESSION

FF1

Blues Talk: *Had a case of the blues just the other night.*
So I played minor 3rds till the mornin' light.
Made me feel all right, like a real good friend.
So I kept on playin' till the moon rose again.

These left-hand bass patterns use a **minor 3rd.**

Woodshed each, then play them by memory

The Walking Bass

Steady moderate beat

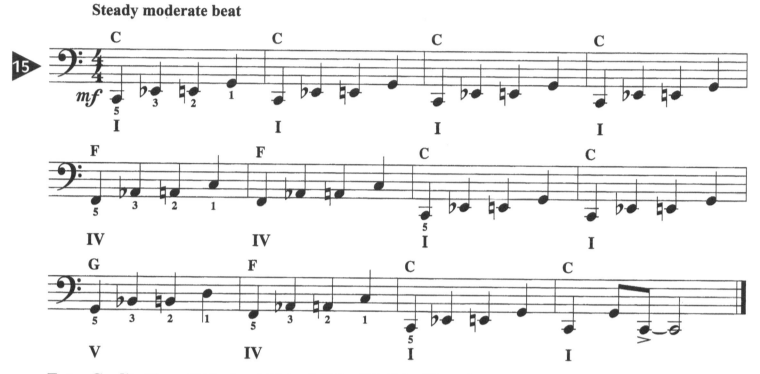

Extra Credit: Play a R.H. chord (C for **I**, F for **IV**, G for **V**) on *beat 1* of each measure.

Hint: First practice slowly for
smooth hand position changes.

The Stomp

Rather fast

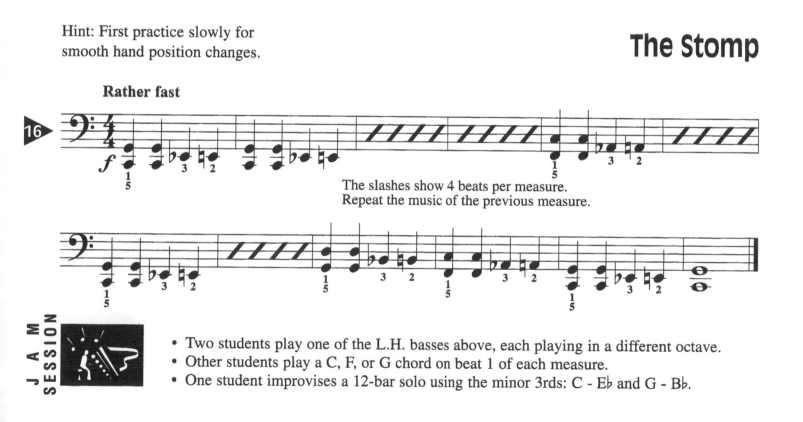

The slashes show 4 beats per measure.
Repeat the music of the previous measure.

- Two students play one of the L.H. basses above, each playing in a different octave.
- Other students play a C, F, or G chord on beat 1 of each measure.
- One student improvises a 12-bar solo using the minor 3rds: C - E♭ and G - B♭.

1155

5-Note Blues Scale in C

The C *blues scale* begins with the C - E♭ minor 3rd, then steps up to G.

Play slowly to help you find the keys.

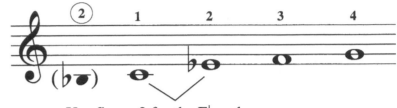

Use finger 2 for the E♭ and for crossing over to B♭.*

1. Play the C blues scale below moving up in octaves.
Memorize the notes and the fingering.

Slow, moderate, then fast swing

mf

Continue playing in higher octaves.

Naming Scale Steps

The steps of the blues scale can be numbered:

- **B♭** is step "flat 7"
- **G** is step 5
- **F** is step 4
- **E♭** is step "flat 3"
- **C** is scale step 1

Blues Scale Steps in C

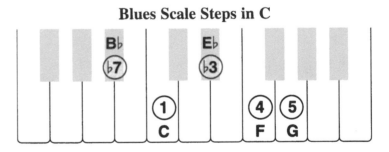

2. Write the letter name and scale step number for these notes from the C blues scale.

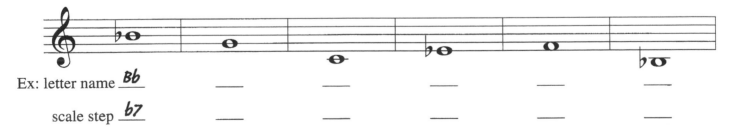

Ex: letter name __B♭__ ___ ___ ___ ___ ___

scale step __♭7__ ___ ___ ___ ___ ___

*__Teachers Note:__ The 1 2 3 4 fingering prepares the student for the 6-note blues scale to follow.
It is the preferred fingering for building speed with the blues scale.

Riff — a short musical pattern.

Playing a *riff* is like speaking a short sentence using notes instead of words.

Play these riffs, for example:

Copycat Riffs will give you a chance to hear and imitate blues riffs.

- Your teacher will play a riff below.
  (You may watch your teacher's hand as you listen.)

- **Play back** what you hear (one octave higher).

Copycat Riffs

Teacher Riffs: (Play in any order.)

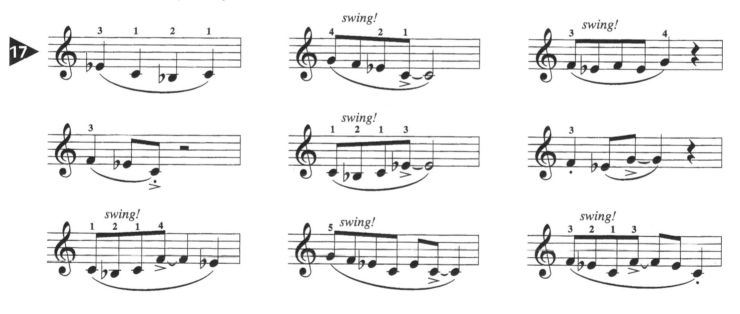

Extra Credit: Try improvising your own riffs. Your teacher may copy them back.

Optional Teacher Bass:

The teacher may play this bass throughout *Copycat Riffs*.

- Students form a line beside the teacher at the piano.
- Teacher plays the repeating L.H. bass throughout the "jam session." Students may clap on beats 2 and 4.
- Play *Copycat Riffs* with the first student. After several imitations, the student moves to the end of the line, and the next student moves to the keyboard.
  Hint: Teacher should keep the bass rhythm going while students are changing places.

Imagine you have just burned a delicious piece of cinnamon toast.

Use the notes of the C blues scale to improvise a right-hand solo for *Burnt Toast Blues*.

Burnt Toast Blues

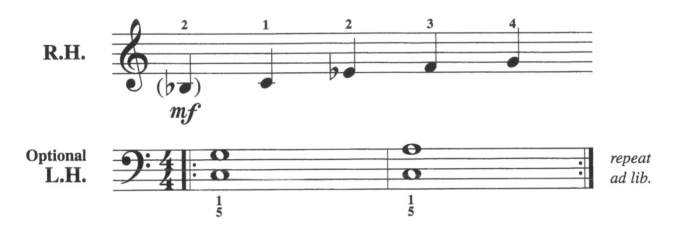

How to Play . . .

At the lesson:

While your teacher plays the duet below, *improvise* with your R.H. alone.
Use the notes of the C blues scale shown above, in any order.

At home:

Begin by playing 4 measures of the left hand alone counting aloud, "1-2-3-4."
Bring in your right hand, *improvising* with any notes of the **C blues scale**.

Hint: Try putting a rest on *beat 1* of every measure for your right hand.
This will make it easier to keep 4 beats per measure.

At first it may be difficult to play hands together. Be patient and keep woodsheddin'!

Optional Ensemble Part (for second keyboard):

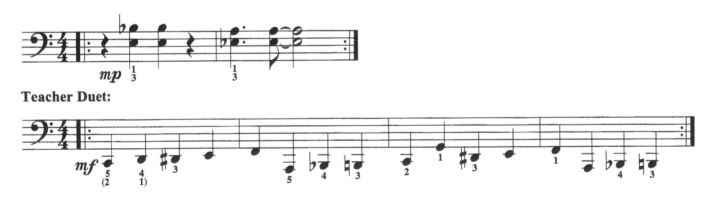

Teacher Duet:

Play *Burnt Toast Blues* as an ensemble. Assign the following parts to one or more students:
- an improvised solo
- the L.H. part (or I and IV chords)
- the optional ensemble part played in any octave
- teacher plays the duet part

Adding the ♭5 to the C Blues Scale

The **flatted 5th** is a "blue note"
which can be added to the blues scale.

(It can also be called a **sharped 4th**.)

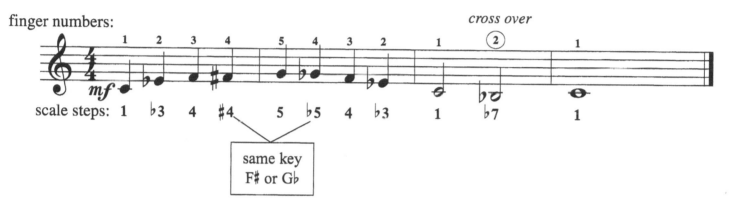

MEMORIZE this C blues scale with the flatted 5th.

Play slowly, letting your fingers *feel* the keys.

Play this exercise at the two tempos shown.

Notice how the tempo can affect the mood
and lyrics of the blues.

Two Blue Moods

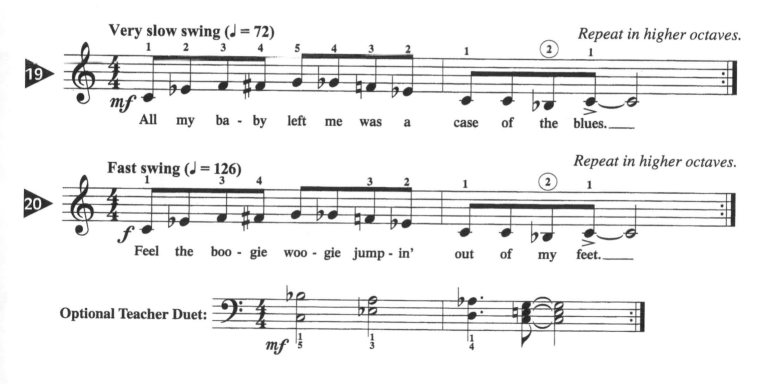

Weather Report Blues follows the 12-bar blues chord progression.

Write a Roman numeral **I**, **IV**, or **V** in each box below the staff.

Practice the piece feeling the *mood* of each tempo below:

slow and soulful (♩ = 96) Weather Report: cold, rainy weather

moderate groove (♩ = 108) Weather Report: clouds, with occasional sunshine

fast swing (♩ = 138) Weather Report: sunny and hot beach weather!

Improvisation: For measures 13-20, use the C blues scale to improvise "atmospheric weather conditions."

Weather Report Blues

N. and R. Faber

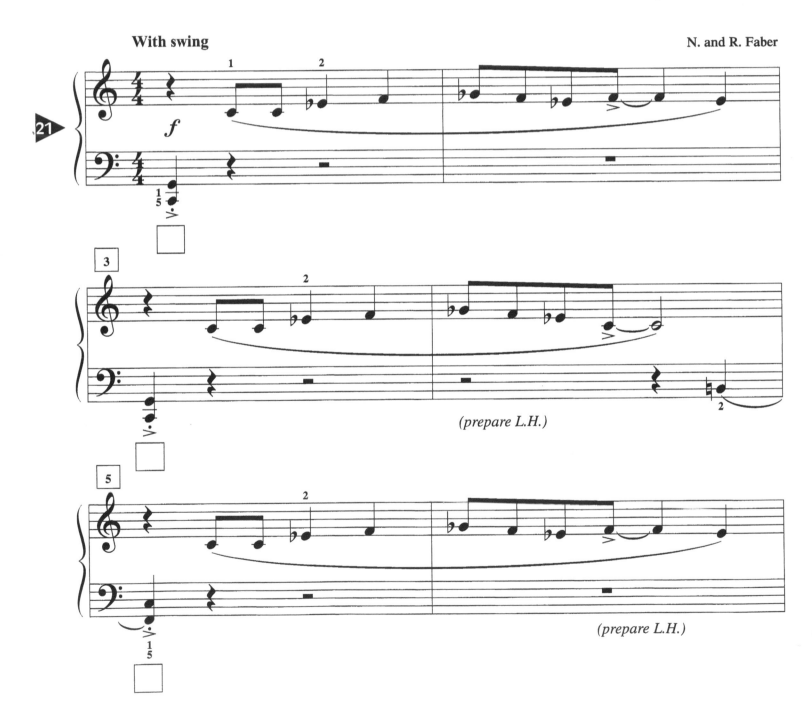

FF1

(The rhythms given are optional, but may be helpful in keeping 4 beats per measure.)

Improvise using notes of the C blues scale above.

Improvise using notes of the C blues scale above.

Form a *Weather Report Team* doing the following:
- One or more students play the bass in lower octaves.
- One or students play the melody in higher octaves.
- For measures 13-20, one student improvises a "blue weather" solo.

Two Blues Hand Positions

Find and play the two positions
for the blues scale as shown.

For each position, finger 2 moves
up a minor 3rd:
C to E♭ and G to B♭.

Practice using the flatted 5th (or ♯4) to cross-over between the two positions.

Play in higher octaves

Put an X on all the keys that are in the **C blues scale**.

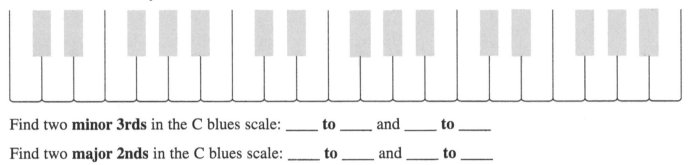

Find two **minor 3rds** in the C blues scale: _____ to _____ and _____ to _____

Find two **major 2nds** in the C blues scale: _____ to _____ and _____ to _____

Riff Corner

Woodshed these riffs until you've "got the chops"! Your teacher will help you.

This improvisation features the left-hand "stomp" that you learned on page 15.

Play it with **straight 8th notes** for a driving "rhythm and blues."

Improvise **8th note riffs** with your
R.H. during the L.H. "breaks."

Use notes from the C blues scale.

Alligator Swamp Stomp

Rather fast, no swing

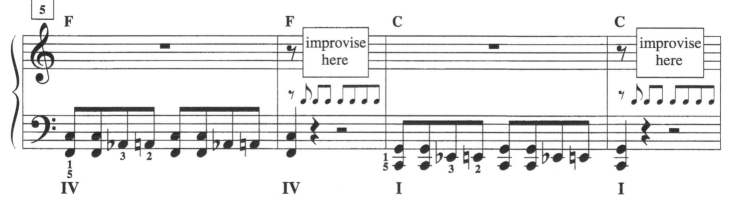

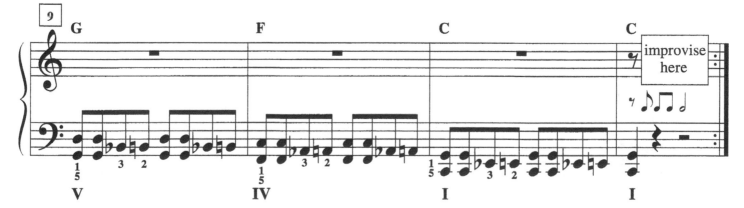

Passing the solo
- A soloist improvises once or twice through the 12 bar blues.
- During the last measures he/she calls out a name, announcing the next soloist.
- (Other students play the L.H. stomp bass or R.H. chords—C, F, G.)

1155

23

A **call and answer** is like a musical conversation.

CALL ⟶ ANSWER

a phrase or riff which asks a question	a second phrase or riff which responds to the call

Parallel Answer

Exact *imitation* is one type of "answer" (as explored in *Copycat Riffs* on page 17).

An answer which imitates the beginning of the call but then ends differently is called a **parallel answer**. A parallel answer will often end on scale step 1.

Play this *call* and *parallel answer*.

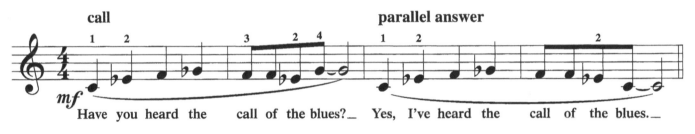

Blues Conversation

Play each *call*. Listen as your teacher follows with a *parallel answer*.
Then reverse roles, and YOU make up a parallel answer.

At home: Practice playing both the call and answer.

24

C Blues Scale Warm-up

Remember the two hand positions: thumb on C or thumb on G.

swing the 8ths!

Improvise a *parallel answer* for each call.
Follow the rhythm given.

Call of the Blues

N. and R. Faber

Moderately, with swing

call   *parallel answer*

Have you heard the   call of the blues?__   Yes, I've heard the   call of the blues.__

call   *parallel answer*

Have you felt the   sigh of the blues?__   Yes, I've felt the   sigh of the blues.__

call   *parallel answer*

Have you played the   sounds of the blues?__ Oh, yes, I play the   blues-i-est blues!

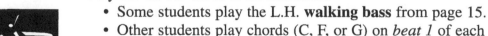

Play the 12-bar blues as an ensemble.
- Some students play the L.H. **walking bass** from page 15.
- Other students play chords (C, F, or G) on *beat 1* of each measure.
- A soloing student improvises **3 calls** and **parallel answers** for the 12-bars.
  A new student solos for the next 12 bars.

J A M S E S S I O N

Contrasting Answer

The *contrasting answer* does not begin like the call.
It may have different notes, different rhythm, or both!

Say the words aloud as you clap the rhythm.
Then play this *call* and *contrasting answer.*

With swing

call

contrasting answer

mf

What's for din - ner, what's for din - ner, tell me please? Cold meat - loaf and lit - tle green peas.

Now improvise your own **contrasting answer** after your teacher plays the **call**.

At home: Play both the call and answer.
Try writing your favorite answers below.

Cold Meatloaf Blues

26 ▶ a.

call

contrasting answer

mf 8 A. M., now what's to eat?__ Two po - ta - toes and one red beet.

b.

call

contrasting answer

mf

12 P. M., what's cook - in' for lunch? Bar - be - cue beans and on - ions to munch.

c.

call *swing the 8ths!* *contrasting answer*

What's for din - ner, what's for din - ner, tell me please? Cold meat - loaf and lit - tle green peas.

J A M S E S S I O N

- Students play the **call** in unison while saying the words aloud.
- One student **improvises an answer** while the group provides "back up" by saying the lyric aloud.
- Repeat with different students improvising the contrasting answer.

FF1

Blues
Ear Training

Listen Up!

At the lesson: Your teacher will play *Blues Band Jam.*
Improvise a *contrasting answer* to follow each call.

At home:

- Play only the **teacher part**, as a solo.

- For a challenge, try improvising your own
  calls to replace the *calls* that are written.

Blues Band Jam

R. Faber

Students play the teacher part as a group. A soloist improvises contrasting answers.
Blues Challenge: Two students play a duet. One improvises the calls, the other
improvises the answers. (Other students may accompany, playing
the bass part for *Blues Band Jam.*)

Exploring Sevenths

Blues Talk: *"I know with the blues I'll be a hit*
When I can find 7ths lickety-split!"

The 7th

The **interval of a 7th** can be major or minor.
The blues uses the interval of a **minor 7th**.
A minor 7th is a **whole step below the octave**.

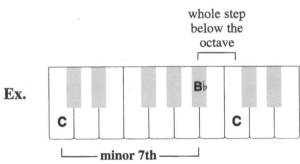

whole step
below the
octave

Ex.

1. Play a **minor 7th UP** from each of these notes. Use L.H. fingers 5 - 1.
Write in the name of the upper note.

Ex.   C to _Bb_   F to ____   G to ____   D to ____

More Barrelhouse Bass

2. "Woodshed" this L.H. pattern until you can play it by memory.

JAM SESSION

• One group plays *More Barrelhouse Bass*.
• The other group plays steady quarter-note chords (C, F, or G) to the 12-bar blues.
• Students take turns improvising solos using the C blues scale.

FF1

Blues Technique

Woodsheddin'

The **triplet** ♪♪♪ rhythm is common in the blues.

Tap this rhythm with your teacher. Use both hands, saying the words aloud.
Hint: Tap at a **slow, moderate,** and **rather fast** tempo.

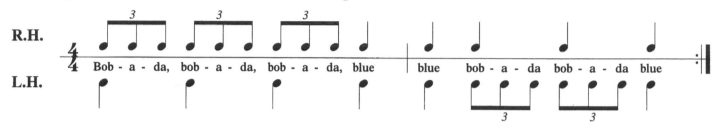

R.H.

Bob - a - da, bob - a - da, bob - a - da, blue   blue   bob - a - da bob - a - da blue

L.H.

Practice at a slow, medium, then fast tempo.
Enjoy the sound of triplets!

Bob-a-da Blues

R. Faber, McLean

Moving along

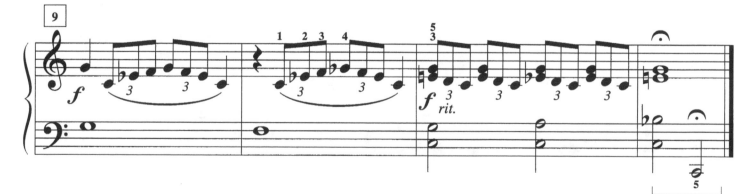

Extra Credit: Can you play *Bob-a-da Blues* with the R.H. playing **one octave higher**?

The Turnaround

When repeating the 12-bar blues, the *last measure* is usually changed to a **V chord**.

This is called a **turnaround**. The V chord leads to the I chord, beginning the 12-bar blues again.

Write **I**, **IV**, or **V** in the boxes below.
Then circle measure 24, the *turnaround*.

"Everything but the Kitchen Sink" Blues

N. Faber

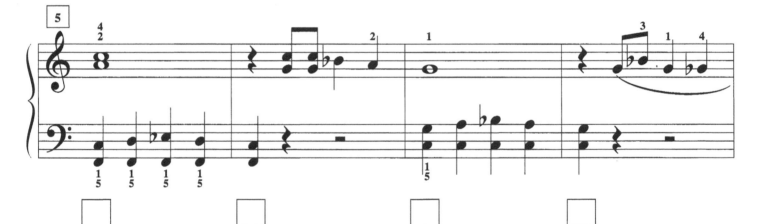

FF11

Improvisation (The rhythms given are optional, but may be helpful in keeping 4 beats per measure.)

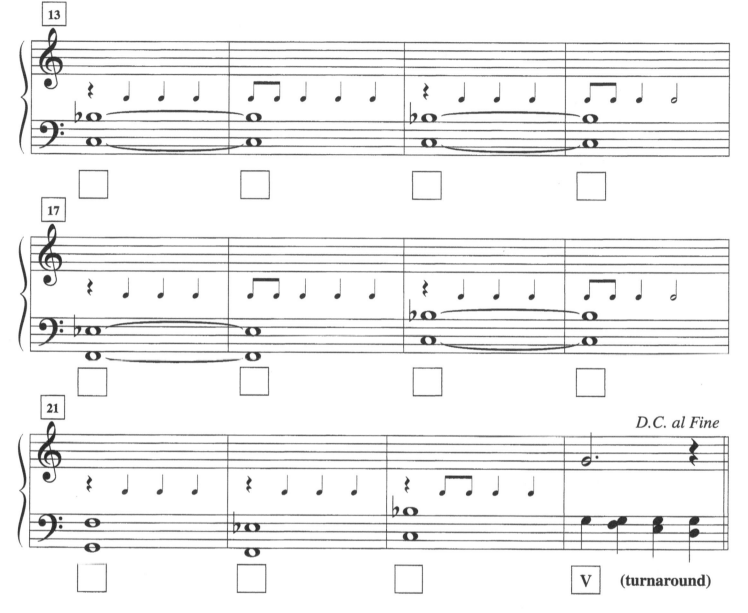

Extra Credit: You may wish to write your favorite improvisation on the staff.

Optional Bass Part for Improvisation Section (mm. 13-24):
(for teacher or class use)

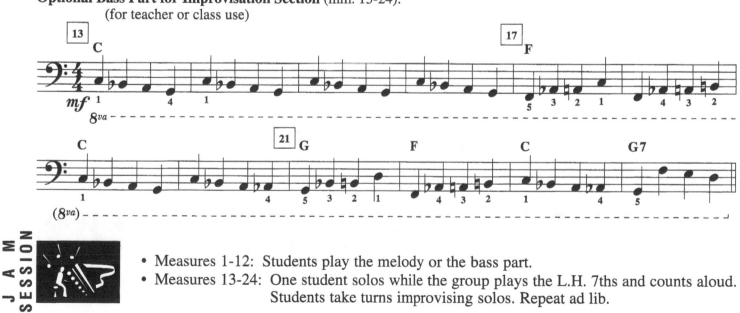

- Measures 1-12: Students play the melody or the bass part.
- Measures 13-24: One student solos while the group plays the L.H. 7ths and counts aloud. Students take turns improvising solos. Repeat ad lib.

REVIEW: The 12-bar blues uses 3 chords—**I, IV, V.**

NEW: In the key of G, these 3 chords are G, C, and D major.

Play the chords below with your left hand.
Say aloud, **"I chord," "IV chord,"** or **"V chord."**

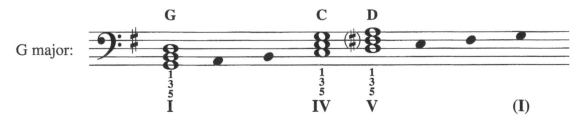

G major:

Label the **I, IV,** and **V**
chords in the boxes below.

Barrelhouse Blues in G

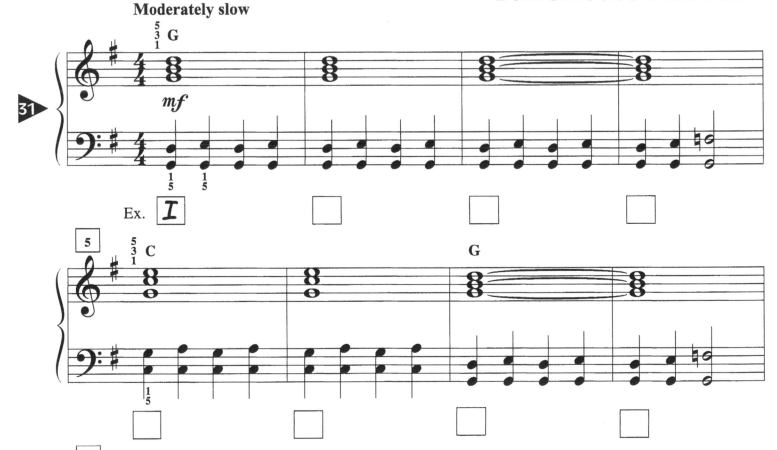

Moderately slow

Ex. I

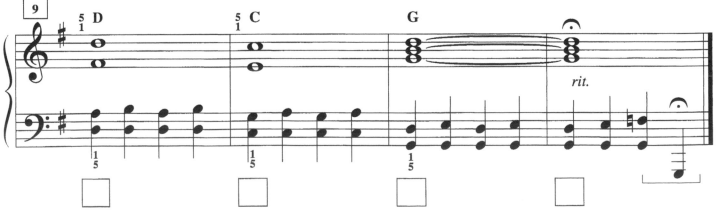

FF11

Mike's Magic Bass uses the *walking bass* in the key of G.

- Before playing, write the chord letter names.

- Woodshed the L.H. alone, especially the
  turnaround back to measure 1.

- Then add the rhythmic R.H. chords.

Mike's Magic Bass

Walking Bass in G

Moderately

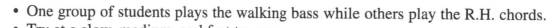

- One group of students plays the walking bass while others play the R.H. chords.
- Try at a slow, medium, and fast tempo.

The Blues Scale in G

1. Learn and memorize the notes and
fingering for the **G blues scale.**

Scale steps: **1   ♭3   4   ♯4   5   ♭5   4   ♭3   1   ♭7   1**

Repeat in higher octaves.

2. Memorize these two hand positions
for the G blues scale.

└─1st hand position─┘   └─2nd hand position─┘

Continue in higher octaves.

3. Put an X on all the keys that are in the **G blues scale.**

4. Where are the **minor 3rds** in the G blues scale? ____ **to** ____   **and**   ____ **to** ____

5. Write the letter name and scale step number for these notes from the **G blues scale.**

Ex. letter name _Db_   ____   ____   ____   ____

scale step _♭5_   ____   ____   ____   ____

FF1

Whiz Kid Warm-up

Practice this **G blues scale** at slow, medium, and fast tempos.

Repeat playing in
higher octaves.

Do you remember *Alligator Swamp Stomp* (p. 23)
in the key of C? Here it is in the key of G.

Improvise your R.H. during the L.H. "breaks."
Use notes from the G blues scale.

Whiz Kid Stomp

Stomp Bass in G

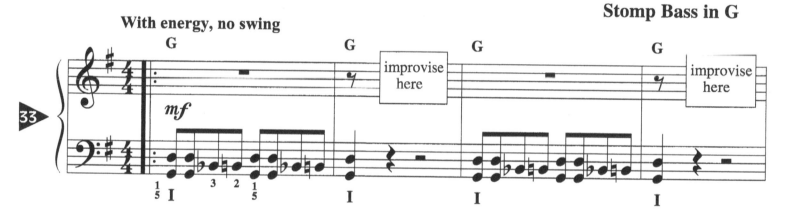

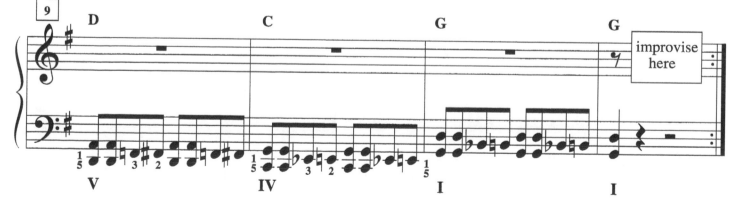

The Agent's Data (from stolen microchip)

- The L.H. uses a **5th-6th-7th-6th** pattern.
- The R.H. uses any notes from the G blues scale.
- Play with straight or swing rhythm.

Secret Agent Blues

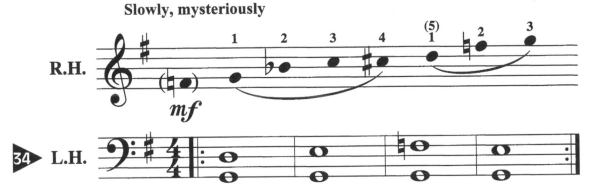

The Agent's Instructions . . .

At Headquarters (the lesson):

While your teacher plays the bass duet below, *improvise* with your R.H. alone.
Use the notes of the G blues scale shown above, in any order.

In your Hideaway (at home):

Introduce the secret agent by playing 4 measures of L.H. alone.
Bring in your R.H. *improvising* with any of the notes of the G blues scale.

Hint: Try putting a rest on *beat 1* of every measure for your right hand.
This will make it easier to keep 4 beats per measure.

Teacher Bass Duet (or for class use):

Optional Treble Part (for class use):

Assign 3 parts to the ensemble:
1) the L.H. Student Part, 2) the Teacher Bass Duet (taught by rote), 3) the Optional Treble Part
Begin with 8 measures of ensemble only. A student soloist then begins improvising.

FF11

Listen Up!

Your teacher will play a blues example which will end on a **5th, 6th,** or **7th.**
Close your eyes and *listen.* **Circle the LAST interval you hear.**

a. 5th   **b.** 5th   **c.** 5th

6th   6th   6th

7th   7th   7th

d. 5th   **e.** 5th   **f.** 5th

6th   6th   6th

7th   7th   7th

For Teacher Use Only

The examples may be repeated several times and played in any order.

- The teacher continues the above drill, making up more blues examples.
- The class may answer verbally, or write the last interval heard on the board.
  (5th, 6th, or 7th)

Blues Technique
Woodsheddin'

Hot Riffs

Practice these riffs with your R.H. alone. (Use swing.)
Transpose your favorite riff to the key of C.

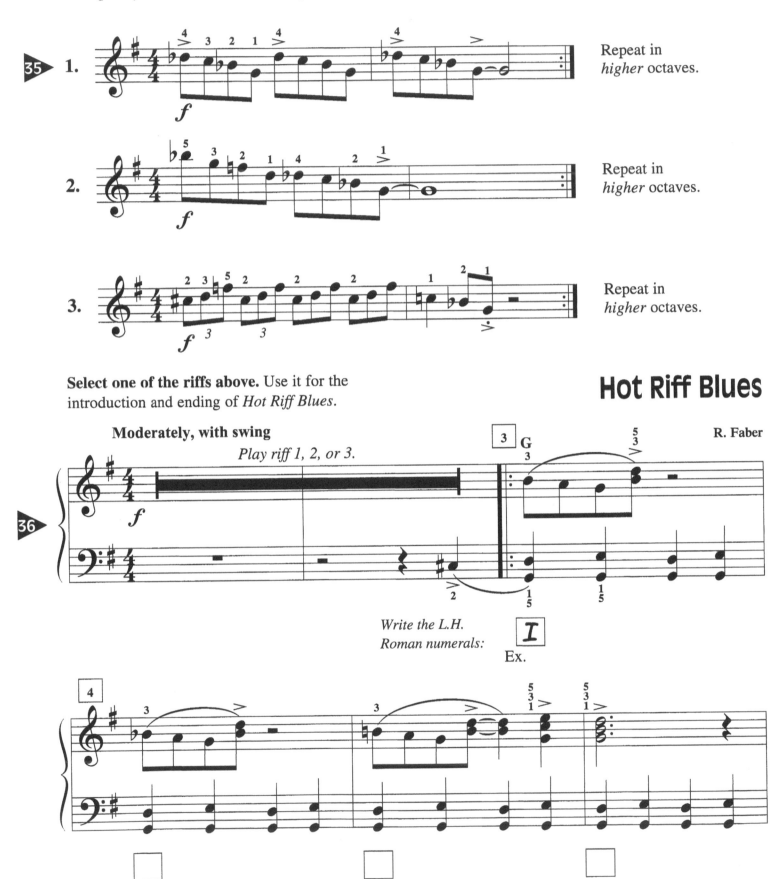

1. Repeat in *higher* octaves.

2. Repeat in *higher* octaves.

3. Repeat in *higher* octaves.

Select one of the riffs above. Use it for the introduction and ending of *Hot Riff Blues*.

Hot Riff Blues

R. Faber

Moderately, with swing

Play riff 1, 2, or 3.

Write the L.H. Roman numerals:

Ex. **I**

FF1

Extra Credit: For the repeat of measures 3-14, try improvising with your right hand.
Use notes from the G blues scale.

- Form a blues ensemble by dividing the treble and bass parts among students.
- A soloist chooses and plays a riff for the introduction and ending.
  Optional repeat of measures 3-14: The soloist improvises using the G blues scale.
  Students playing the treble part now play G, C, and D chords for these 12 bars.

Final Review: "Teach" each of the following musical terms to your teacher.

Dictionary of Musical Terms

TERM	DEFINITION
answer	A phrase which immediately follows a "call."
barrelhouse	A blues piano style with a steady, repeating left-hand pattern.
break	A stop in the accompaniment where only the soloist plays.
call	A phrase or riff which begins a "musical conversation."
contrasting answer	An answering phrase which has different notes or rhythms than the *call*.
half step	From one key to the *very next* key.
imitation	Exact repetition in any octave.
improvise	Create music "on the spot."
interval	The distance between two pitches.
minor 2nd	Half step; the smallest interval on the keyboard (Ex. C - D♭).
major 2nd	Whole step (Ex. C - D); the distance of two half steps.
minor 3rd	Equal to a whole step plus a half step (Ex. C - E♭). The minor 3rd is common in the blues.
major 3rd	Equal to two whole steps (Ex. C - E).
minor 7th	The interval which is a whole step less than an octave (Ex. C - B♭).
parallel answer	An answering phrase which begins like the "call."
progression	Pattern of chords (Ex. I - IV - V - I is a chord progression).
riff	Any short musical pattern used in improvising.
swing rhythm	8th notes played in a long-short pattern.
stomp	A blues style with a driving, rhythmic bass.
straight rhythm	8th notes played evenly.
tempo	"Speed" of the music.
triplet	Three eighth notes which equal a quarter note ($\overset{3}{\flat\flat\flat}$ = ♩).
turnaround	Substitution of the V chord for the last measure (m.12) of the 12-bar blues. The turnaround leads into measure 1 for a repeat of the 12-bars.
walking bass	A bass line which moves by step or chord outline and is played on each beat of the measure.
whole step	Two half steps (2 keys with one key in-between); a major 2nd.
woodshed	Slang expression meaning to practice hard on one's own.
12-bar blues	A repeating 12-measure chord progression that is used in the blues. See page 8 for the basic 12-bar blues chord progression.